OFF THE B

OFF THE BEATEN TRACK

A year in haiku

Christopher Herold
Fabian Ironside
Hamish Ironside
Éireann Lorsung
Bob Lucky
Momus
Matthew Paul
Sally Read
George Swede
Michael Dylan Welch
Matthew Welton
Hugo Williams

BOATWHISTLE BOOKS

First published in 2016
by Boatwhistle Books
10 Princes Road
Teddington
London TW11 0RW
United Kingdom

www.boatwhistle.com

Typeset by Boatwhistle
in Caslon with a hint of Gill Sans

A catalogue record for this book
is available from the British Library

ISBN 978-1-911052-01-2

Printed in the United Kingdom by Short Run Press, Exeter
on 80 gsm Munken Premium paper

2 4 6 8 10 9 7 5 3 1

CONTENTS

JANUARY

Hugo Williams

What we have here
is a gate in a wall
with its timetable of opening hours

Such an old tree
Perhaps he has memories
Of John Clare's moment of fame

The natural world
is shivering and shaking
as if it could see into the future

Not much chance
of getting away this weekend.
But wait, there may be

It's hard work pedalling uphill in the rain,
but after a while I don't seem to mind.
Nothing seems to matter any more

No roads going north
No roads going south
No roads going anywhere

Never mind what you're thinking about,
it's what you're not thinking about
that counts

Writing a haiku
isn't as easy as it looks.
You have to be interrupted all the time

You're writing things down
because you want to.
But suppose you don't want to.

You think blocks of white and grey
on a blue background
are clouds floating across the sky

The word 'salad'
lies across the top
of my first haiku

The toy family glass
and the silk family stone
won't speak to one another

Monday on the bus with Lucas
A poem about unhappiness
written all over his face

Thank you so much for the detective book
I'm going out straight away
to have a look around

The Indian nurse moves slowly back and forth
between the glove dispenser
and the needle disposal box

The old doctor has learned
how to talk to a patient
in his sleep

Basins of soapy water
have arrived in the ward,
nothing else has happened

Washing my hands
a swirl of water down the sink
always darker than you expect

Soap surfs the soap dish
like a baby crocodile.
You have to see it.

It's de white man, announces the male nurse,
wheeling what looks like
a corpse into the ward

A daddy-long-legs
crawling up Noël Coward's face
on the television

Do you drop things?
We drop things all the time
(this includes breaking them)

The stairs are full of nostalgia
We miss the rail we got rid of
when we were young

O darling don't be horrible
Everything is so terrible
I only want to kiss you

See how freely we move about the room
knowing where everything is
making the tea

It's over on the left,
making a noise like the sea.
Oh, it is the sea!

Scraps of dandruff crowd the parting of my student antagonist
Worker ants carrying breadcrumbs to their pregnant queen
Or poems lost in the forest of the imagination?

Don't take any notice
of sudden reverses in fortune
Embrace the velvet hour

If you feel a desire for death
think about the sweet-scented geranium
how it responds to your touch

Good old desk!
How sorry I am to be losing you
On the other hand, what a sweat it all was

Getting ready to go out
time passes quickly
suddenly it's too late

FEBRUARY

Hamish Ironside

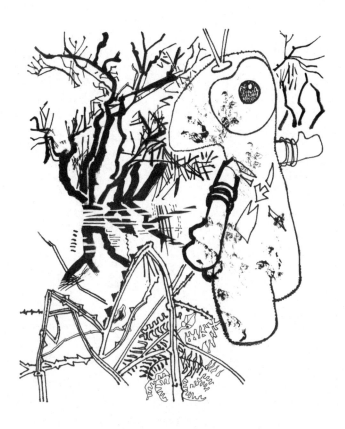

a shabby Wenlock
dangling from a zip—
bleak midwinter

cloud smothering sun . . .
secondguessing
my subconscious

showing them
how it's done—
the mason's grave

the surgeon's wink
just before
I'm under

late winter
coaxing the last ink
from a biro

a swell of starlings
pulled to different trees
leaves a line of air

winter blues—
I trade Hemingway
for Anne Frank

proofing a text
about mindfulness
without reading it

small-town charity shop—
I tell an old lady
I'll never be back

lost in the rain
I smell the sheep reviving
in my jumper

a wren
explores the forest
of a single pine

in the library
laughing all the louder
for the silence

winter morning—
the last pancake
a map of Australia

orange streetlight
shows the grain of wood
in wet paving slabs

first spring sun—
a firehose gushes
into the Thames

Saturday afternoon—
the stress of trying to be
Type B

a fuzzy tannoy
rendered dub poetry
by the busker's reggae

long-distance call—
years fall away
for a few seconds

half-moon
I tell the barista *precisely*
how my day has been

a dream leaves
the aftertaste
of spitting out teeth

buddleia sprouting
from a derelict cinema—
winter's slight return

no one waves back
to the people on the boat
heading out to sea

my brother long gone,
our walk's mark goes on—that one
toenail's cut blue john

the jar of groundscore
raided for the paper . . . well,
what else is it for?

eleven days later
the red rose's
raffish look

'love' written six times
in joined-up pencil
on the sport section

winter touches spring
as the past touches the future—
a gull pursues a heron

a patient's wife
assures a nurse
'everything will come right'

MARCH

Matthew Paul

St David's Day
a coot's wake spans the whole of
the Duke of Northumberland's River

cold rain
my son and I thank the driver
at the same time

over the railway
two ducks synchronize
their rapid descent

Apple Market—
one of those days when
everyone looks familiar

tricks of the light snow that tickles your nose

under the arches
some Tex-Mex buskers
give it some oomph

a pigeon ducks under
the security gate
winter's end

surging wind . . .
the percentage of my run
when I'm off the ground

spring sunlight
in the river's crook
a chorus of crows

night rain
the warmth of her kisses
on my spine

on his phone,
my friend smiles hello
with his eyebrows

first bumblebee
the town gas holder
all but empty

wind-sped flurries
a wagtail scampers out
from the lorry's path

snow-cum-hail
two colleagues flirt
in the open plan

yellow dusk
the crow-chased magpie
returns to its spot

the southerly wind
shakes the eucalyptus—
her old photos

in my eyeline
a green woodpecker
bounces onto the clump

without my glasses
I recognise my son
by his stride

soaked to the skin . . .
the basso profondo of
the loudest crow

evangelicals:
their keyboard-player gives it
the full Rick Wakeman

magpies nest-build—
the smell of school dinners
wafts with the breeze

into the headwind:
the wisps from somebody's
spent cigarette

after each slap of sleet at the window her cheeky grin

within camellia petals:
that's the only place where
the snow has settled

a willy wagtail
flies across the Hogsmill
with one quick bounce

full moon
my mother recalls
the smogs of her youth

my bright idea . . .
the sun in the shingle
dragged back and forth

wild daffodils
a spaniel splashes up
the side channel

my train cancelled—
icicles elongate
the pointy dags

rain turns to sleet
we glimpse from the bus
topiary elephants

painted lady—
the sun's rays slope across
crazy paving

APRIL

Michael Dylan Welch

pinker
against the blue
graveyard cherry blossoms

painterly clouds—
the steering wheel warm
for the first time this spring

rain in the forecast—
what have I done
with my afternoon?

hazy sun—
the rest area sign
says free coffee

burn ban—
a eucalyptus leaf
between my fingers

estate sale—
a dried-up cactus
in the garden shed

coastal drive—
we roll down the windows
to hear the ocean

elbow to elbow
at the poetry reading . . .
her black coffee

a day without rain—
I save the thickest envelope
to open last

old gas station—
one suction cup popped loose
on the closed sign

after the news
the morning paper
still unread

spring sun—
my shaver changes pitch
as I plug it in

graupel in the shadows—
the schoolyard tetherball
twists in the wind

a hearse
up from the valley
wet with blossoms

tax day—
reading glasses left
on the kitchen table

spring cleaning—
tossing out a box
of old business cards

national haiku day—
where's a scrap of paper
when I need it

MICHAEL DYLAN WELCH

moss on the path—
you ask me, quietly,
if I have summer plans

April showers—
a library book
left under an oak

soap bubbles popping
on the lost puppy poster—
inner city park

little league photo day—
mud stains
on the catcher's knees

car trip—
we add new harmonies
to a disco tune

on an old memory card
a photo of my sister
in her chemo wig

the ferry quiets
as it drifts in to dock—
rising moon

sapwood—
I learn something new
about my mother

a stand of larch—
the towhee tells me
to go home

new neighbours—
the story again
of the wasp nest

poetry reading—
I hear nothing more
after he says loam

national anthem—
the bald coach
removes his cap

extra innings—
she goes on telling me
about her divorce

MAY

Matthew Welton

low cloud, cold toast
too much coffee
in the coffee

apricot tree
blossom the colour
of lichen

birdless back yard—
too early to be
this awake

nettles beneath
the raspberry canes
pebbles and slugs

the poplars
perpendicular
to their shadows

slow clouds, slow winds
paracetamol
and coffee

breakfast table
beer bottle
radiator heat

among the weeds
the onions
barely even green

a lemon on
the breadboard
a trickle of juice

tree-colour sparrow
in the
sparrow-colour tree

dusky morning
the weak coffee
and the headache

sudden cloud
and sudden sunlight
wasps at the milk

empty tumbler
empty tumbler
empty tumbler

warm rain
on the warm pavement—
ferret on a lead

spindly branches
tangled between
telegraph wires

in the rain
the teenager
running up to bowl

a grapefruit on
a table
the trickle of juice

slow breeze
deep cloud
electric mower in the rain

flimsy poppies
in the flimsy wind—
low pale sun

picnic bench breakfast
milky coffee
milky clouds

their shadows
perpendicular
to the poplars

cloudy morning
coffee
refrigerator hum

dozing on the steps
harmonica
in his hand

and the shadow
of the stack
of unreturned books

crabapple tree
lichen the colour
of blossom

sullen cloud
and sullen sunlight
wasps in the sink

kitchen counter—
the jam jar
entirely empty

our shadows
ride home on
the shadows of our bikes

alone on the lawn
with dandelions
in his hands

picnic bench breakfast
cloudy coffee
cloudy skies

sunlight through
the kitchen door
and i can't get warm

JUNE

Christopher Herold

farmer's market
a pair of butterflies whirls
above the fiddlers

wind riffles
    the neighbor's magnolia
sailboats on the bay

dense fog
the horizon unrolls white
on the beach

lighthouse
the semi-circular sweep
of coastal fog

sand fleas swarm
the carcass of a seal
beach party

moonless night
moths beat their wings
on my candlelit tent

alone tonight
the flams and paradiddles
of rain on the roof

Persian carpet
the cat grooms kitty-litter
from between its toes

cracks in the concrete
      of a gun-emplacement
dandelions

public restroom
asparagus overwhelms
the urinal cake

a long flight of steps
dark clouds come slowly
over the hill

humid afternoon
a painted lady lands
on the windbell

rural tavern
a row of suspenders
at the bar

low-slung clouds
    scud across the bay
cilantro bolting

hillside crisscrossed
 with barbed wire fences
wildflowers

my daughter calls
 to ask me a favor
Father's Day

moss-covered stumps
 under the forest canopy
 the patter of rain

alpine lake
a fisherman casts
into morning mist

dry streambed
ferns under the footbridge
rippled by wind

stretching
   my imagination
Venus flytrap

the longest day
a tugboat tows a barge
towards the rising moon

throat-tickle
twigs scrape across
the zendo window

bee sting
my thoughts return
to the present

snowy owl
the moon slices pathways
through the woods

sick room
the walls brighten and dim
with the passing of clouds

zazen outside
a few notes from the wind bell
as the sun sets

hot afternoon
a breeze in the shadow
of one small cloud

cauliflower clouds
I unroll my sleeping bag
in the open

paper lampshade
winged silhouettes disappear
into the light

totem pole
rain dripping from beaks,
from eyes

JULY

Sally Read

The night is empty.
Birdsong fills it like water,
a shard of water.

Dawn leaves tremble,
nourished by silence and dark:
Your tender violence.

Brown jasmine blossom
is trailed through the house.
We walk on dry offerings.

Her red dress flickers
against the pale sea,
igniting the last edge of dusk.

Fireflies float like unmanned boats—
only the pull
of coupling to steer them.

In the tabernacle
the host is steady, lightless
as a beating heart.

Early morning air,
pure as neat vodka.
It blurs the emerald pines.

Bright, slamming heat!
The girl in the orange dress
is a black shape, distant.

As the rain breaks through,
smell rises from soft roads.
Tongues out, we are doused embers.

Sea blanches, darkens,
at the sky's penetrating touch.
So, I would mirror You.

Evening, lamp posts
throw down long, low shadows
in exhausted adoration.

Now she sleeps—a cartwheel
of starlings sucked back
into the arms of a tree.

I wake to glass beads
cascading onto the floor:
crickets rattling my dreams.

A silent, black sea.
The ship's a blazing city!
Blunt as Mary's angel.

The hot hour. Her face
smooth as a dish of water
waiting for a breath.

From far out at sea
people on the shore
chirrup, busy as birds on bread.

Evening, the dry grass
unburdens itself of scent,
like a lover.

Slippery gold plum flesh
won't be ripped from its black stone.
Lord, come into my heart.

In the night's collapsed dark
the long slam of a goods train
gathering my blood.

The quiet sea is scentless.
Young men stand on rocks: paintings
on a cave wall.

The poor man squats
with a basket of shells
writing names of the rich on each one.

To You I'm a firefly,
my skin so thin I show all
that burns and dies in me.

Grown-ups all sleeping.
Cicadas sanding their wings.
The clock's tick is lost.

Black snake cut in two,
the mosaic skin cringes loose—
it was never his.

Bird trapped in the dome,
flinging its small bones,
is blind to the open window.

This is my body . . .
Tiny black wings freight the church:
one cicada sings.

Under the lip of sleep
You are there—loud as dreams—
a tale, long under way.

        Cicadas wheezing,
        cello climbing through my skin.
        The house still empty.

    The blackbird's singing
    of winter lanes, and Your sweet
    occupation of me.

There was rain in the first hours.
The garden arched its back.
Refreshed, she slept on.

Her small hand in mine,
the old road from church to sea.
Christ lodged in my teeth.

AUGUST

George Swede

traffic jam . . .
juxtapositions jostle
for the open lane

an uprising
of rebellious thoughts—
no coherent third line

doubt become
an object of itself—
vine-wrapped oak

naming is
not understanding—
dazzling sunset

a neighbour's loud music
keeps the page blank—the float
of dandelion puffs

GEORGE SWEDE

under the fridge
glass shards, tangled dust—
our archived lives

packed subway . . .
a burp from
the tinned sardine lunch

missing little girl—
the bottom of the poster
flaps in the wind

archeological dig—
as sand streams from a skull
grinding thoughts

horizon moon—
the yappy dog bigger
than it sounds

campsite's carbon footprint
a moth flutters over my
tepee of kindling

her morning smile . . .
sunbeams across the terrain
of my cortex

rainy season break . . .
the streets full of people
in fast forward

ripening field tomatoes . . .
the baby bumps of two
migrant workers

meadow wildflowers   definitely cremation

climate change heat
lucky ant lingers under
a blade of grass

storm over . . .
the tattered cobweb
nets a fly

family circle—
i choose words with
the letter o

wind
on water . . .
the days

waiting for
the yeast to rise . . .
stock market low

the stray dog
the corner beggar
eyeing each other

historical novel—
i now notice the alley's
scent of urine

new tendrils as the
vine's leaves yellow—
gnarled fingers on the pen

laneway milkweed
for the monarchs . . .
just buzzing flies

faded garden . . .
the turn of the
notebook page

at dawn and now dusk
a mist from the ferment of
the changing seasons

out of the mist
into high country . . .
a view of the mist

silver lace blooms
the bee drone
autumnal

midnight bell tolls . . .
i recall the crunch of last year's
first fallen leaves

the morning paper—
thirty-one the ways i've seen
the oak this August

the who i really am
increasingly apparent—
laugh lines

SEPTEMBER

Bob Lucky

rainy season chill
policemen on the edge
of the demonstration

first-period bell
student slug trails crisscross
the dewed grass

dark night even darker potholes

rain clouds
the harsh laugh of ibis
overhead

false banana plant
in the beer garden a man
claims to know me

approaching dusk
a hamerkop's squishy
landing on the green

chewing *chat*—
never again, I said
the first time

evening shower
the silence my son left
returning to school

flat tire
the ping of fat raindrops
on the hood

waiting for coffee . . .
the back and forth
of weaver birds

New Year's Day
surrounded by girls
drumming for money

thunder storm
my wife falls asleep
on the couch again

scattered starlight
the crispness of pizza
baked over a fire

hazy moonlight
I find my songbook
of two-chord tunes

chanting from the church
the sheep's head outside the gate
almost something else

drowned out
by the downpour
the silence between us

rush hour traffic
a man with a dozen roses
takes his chances

yellow dahlias
a smear of sunrise
across the wall

cold in my bones
wishing I felt as young
as this single malt

no rain today
my wife's blood thinner
than it used to be

sudden squall
we don't go home
the way I would go

autumn equinox
her side of the bed
and mine

anniversary
the impatiens bursting
to bloom

grey skies
my decision to give up
sugar

cloudless morning
a Meskel flower tucked
behind my ear

warm afternoon
just enough breeze
to sway the teff

losing faith . . .
a whiff of benzine
in the *demera*'s flames

cascades of dust
on the road
to the Blue Nile Falls

a pied wagtail
de-wings a dragonfly
last day of break

looking for the words . . .
the cloudless sky a tangle
of hawking kites

OCTOBER

Momus

Uncoated
Would look terrible because of
The paper stock. So matte.

They talk about going
To New York
But will probably stay in Berlin.

He failed in art because he was
Too proud
To suck Klaus Biesenbach's cock.

I know so little about
Where my sister is now,
Why, and with whom.

A harpsichord might taste
Like an orange
If it was a citrus fruit.

A ghastly green parody of you!
I am blushing
Like a lobster.

Bees, fish, smoke,
LED-faced men.
Here I get good ideas for my book.

As storms are predicted
For this afternoon
I'm a little teapot.

Is there a gas leak?
The bubble tea girl says:
'No, it's the durian!'

We gather here to scatter
The ashes
Of footballer Betty Page.

Faux-English accents.
Herculaneum is tons better
Than Pompeii.

Quai de Branly.
You are a mother
And your job is divination.

Sounds of motorscooters, church bells
And caged birds.
It's warmer than Paris.

His girlfriend sends him
Angry texts the whole time
And he smokes heavily.

A warm build of empathy
Becomes
A Vesuvial erection.

A typhoon
Sounds exciting
As long as you aren't flying in a plane.

Deliver us
O Lord
From the Morrissey autobiography!

Inflatable toes and eggs.
An Asian beauty
Seen from front and back.

Nuclear nightmare
Prepared by the Atomic
Sciences Committee.

Poetry Europe series:
Shadow Land by
Johannes Bobrowski.

Aunt Molly can't remember
The start of sentences
Dad can't finish.

Just x more Vine videos
And y more tweets
And we'll have the whole thing!

I thought they'd switched
To the euro here
But it seems they still use zlotys.

She didn't like the Currie boys
Despite wide grins like
The Kennedys.

'Dog maul flashbacks haunt our Broagan'
And other headlines
From sad Glasgow.

He fell
Seconds after I snapped,
The window-cleaner at the Westin.

Warsaw!
Thank God for 'the north'
And all its careful organisation.

                    I've forgotten the name
                    I call my penis!
                    A sign of Alzheimer's?

Such people are always pursuing
Scenester Audrey
Hepburn-type girls.

Three hours sitting
Looking at my Facebook page
Passive–aggressively.

Ex-blogger? Fine.
It'll be a sad day when I'm an ex-
Selfie queen.

NOVEMBER

Fabian Ironside

Better-looking version
Of my dermatologist.
Fourteenth & Sixth.

A finger puppet
Of the current president
On the bookshop floor.

A strange city.
Unsure how to use
The subway turnstile.

Eating food before
Paying at supermarket.
But from the buffet?

Gloomy Chicago.
Hotel umbrella the size
Of a katana.

A skyscraper lost
In the low cluster of clouds.
Galactus, his leg.

Chicago evening,
Turned into my mother—
Ordered starter as a main.

Green Mill Cocktail Lounge.
Blind organist hails in song
Everyone but us.

Unutterable
Disappointment on completing
Lego model.

The epic film about
The Great Awakening
Will never be made.

Japanese waiter
Defiantly speaks English
To his countrymen.

Veterans' Day, Fifth Ave.
Three cops in golf buggy.
Back seat: Rodin's Thinker.

My brother's call—
Sudden urgent need to know,
'Did Oswald act alone?'

Mitch Miller album,
Sentimental Moods. Been on
The floor for months now.

After twenty years
He renamed *The Time Machine*
'*Mystery Island.*'

Books I can't sell
Nor give away. Monograph on
Fenimore Cooper.

Fudging details
In story of Thoreau, Alcott
And Whitman's mother.

Mohamed Morsi
In court. Suit *sans* tie—
The Saddam Hussein look.

Day laborer
Dozing on subway, cupping cock:
Millet's Angelus.

Who are they, the old
Men lurking in bank foyers.
'They shall come no more.'

The great man is dead
But his works shall endure:
His advert for headphones.

Getting near sundown.
Baleful expressions from the
Clerks in the bike shop.

Tip of island, dusk:
Black militant Muslim,
His patent light blue scrubs.

Selling books, Strand.
Worst dread realized:
'Fred will be your buyer today.'

Husband and wife
Swooning over photos of
His mother when young.

Subway breakdancers.
Always contrive to invade
The car where I hide.

The lady runner's
Utility belt—all this
For a three-mile jog?

'Wrong from the start,' I
Diligently brushed my teeth
Then ate an orange.

'A man with a dildo
In his hand looks effeminate!'
'What? Did I err?'

Self-consciously literary man
Brings his own mug
To the coffee house.

DECEMBER

Éireann Lorsung

Nothing in the dark
except December,
some small lights

Shaking the tree:
an earwig, a spider;
the mice have gone

How good & cool
water tastes, waking
too warm at night

The smell of pine
through the house:
sap like flames

White hyacinth—
tin can; tea—
my oldest mug

In low yellow fields
two horses reveling
in new-laid hay

Fog in the morning
then the sun, pink,
& neighbor's fields

Swans fly the Leie:
unfrozen, clear & cold
it doubles them

No frost on fields—
I turn earth, I bring
wood in for a fire

Stark light, last leaf;
the sycamore's pods
shake against blue

Thin branch:
yellow leaves
three golden coins

ÉIREANN LORSUNG

Blue descending
everywhere—room
we all live in, darkly

Tea steaming
in the still-cold house
(morning)

Heiße maronen, he calls
& evening touches us
with light fingers

Neighbors move
in our walls like mice
move in stored grain

Light in windows:
perfect circles
perfect 8-point stars

Nameless flower
by the road—
memory's color

Primrose: mistaken,
too early—yellow
as sunrise in winter

Roof & magpie
& blue—my mouth
full of licorice

Kijk altijd naar wat
onzichtbaar is,
words in twilight

Last summer's berries
in my friend's hands;
my memory, her kitchen

Old hospital
through dry, tall grass—
here, with tea, with you

Four candles, tree,
warmth, spicy food,
a long drive in the dark

My finger traces
the architect's name
in cold stone: 1923

Discarded orchid (white)
on gray pavement;
a grate with iron flowers

At her table:
red candles, thin china,
us in one room again

Rain at night,
courtyard full of talk:
one window's lit

A bulb tossed months ago
in an empty bed
has two bright leaves

Even boiling water
smells good
this morning

Screen door built
last summer: whorls
of frost on it now

Old year, dying:
we, here, with fowl
& beast, dark & light

AFTERWORD

The twelve writers in *Off the Beaten Track* were all set the same challenge: to write one haiku a day for a full calendar month. It was perhaps a perverse challenge, because it was set in the knowledge that the 'strike rate' for haiku can be fairly low. Even for an experienced writer of haiku, there can be an element of trial and error about it that is absent from any other form of writing. And then there is that other problem: some days, nothing much happens.

Yet we thought the promise (or threat) of publication might concentrate the mind into raising the strike rate a little. Moreover, we were especially interested in those days when nothing much happens, even if the resulting haiku for such days were a little 'rougher'. Contradictory as it may seem, the rougher haiku can be more interesting than the 'better' ones, much as the hastily recorded B-side was often more interesting than the more polished A-side in the days of the seven-inch single.

Another important aspect of this writing experiment was the selection of writers. Half of those who took part have written and published a large number of haiku, while the other half are better known for other forms of poetry (or for songwriting and quasi-samizdat literature, in a couple of cases). The latter camp had all written either very few haiku or none at all. The hope was that they would bring to the project the 'beginner's mind' that is traditionally considered an important element of haiku in a more literal, perhaps purer sense than a more experienced *haijin* would be able to. The point of the project, then, was to both juxtapose and integrate the two camps, and in doing so perhaps achieve a little more integration of the currently quite separate worlds of haiku and other forms of literature. So, while this is a book of English-language haiku, it is one that is indeed off the beaten track.

Following the writing part of the project, we sought twelve of the most distinctive artists we could find to provide illustrations for the opening page of each month, each basing their work loosely on one haiku from within that month. The results of both the writing and the illustration have far exceeded any expectations we may have had at the outset. We thank all twenty-four participants for entering so fully into the spirit of the experiment.